WISH MEAL

OTHER TITLES FROM AIRLIE PRESS

THE EDDY FENCE   *Donna Henderson*

LAST APPLES OF LATE EMPIRES   *Jessica Lamb*

GARDEN OF BEASTS   *Anita Sullivan*

OUT OF REFUSAL   *Carter McKenzie*

ENTERING   *Cecelia Hagen*

THE NEXT THING ALWAYS BELONGS   *Chris Anderson*

CONGRESS OF STRANGE PEOPLE   *Stephanie Lenox*

IRON STRING   *Annie Lighthart*

STILL LIFE WITH JUDAS & LIGHTNING   *Dawn Diez Willis*

SKEIN OF LIGHT   *Karen McPherson*

PICTURE X   *Tim Shaner*

PARTLY FALLEN   *Deborah Akers*

SETTING THE FIRES   *Darlene Pagán*

THE CATALOG OF BROKEN THINGS   *A. Molotkov*

For Hannah
with fond appreciation
for your starting
gift.

WISH
MEAL

Tim Whitsel

~~TIM WHITSEL~~

Airlie Book
Launch
2019

Airlie PORTLAND OREGON Press
2016

Airlie Press is supported by book sales, by contributions to the press from its supporters, and by the work donated by all the poet-editors of the press.

Major funding has been provided by, or on behalf of:
Christine Stephenson
Julia Ryan Wills
Anonymous in honor of Ann and Erik Muller

P.O. BOX 82653
PORTLAND OR 97282
WWW.AIRLIEPRESS.ORG

EMAIL: EDITORS@AIRLIEPRESS.ORG

Cover and Book Design: Beth Ford, Glib Communications & Design, Portland, OR

Cover Photo: Todd Quackenbush

FIRST EDITION

ISBN: 978-09895799-4-0

Library of Congress Control Number: 2016937017

Printed in the United States of America

for

—————⹀————— *Gib Whitsel*

who taught me

love

for

this land

All men are by nature free; you have therefore an undoubted liberty to depart whenever you please, but will have many and great difficulties to encounter in passing the frontiers.

 Voltaire,
Candide

Think of the long trip home.
Should we have stayed at home and thought of here?
Where should we be today?

Elizabeth Bishop,
Questions of Travel

CONTENTS

FERMENT

III

FURROW & DRIFT

IV

I

WISH MEAL

RESIDE

Suppose a fibrous leaf plucked
from an everyday plant were ideal
to wipe clean any residue
clinging to the gourd bowl, tannins
sterilizing what sands
from the gravel bar upriver could not scour.
Suppose a man could occupy
the carved laurel stool
in a clearing between five houses
for his morning brew or midday meal
and for the close-at-hand piece-work
by which stories of demons
or ancestors are recited,
fishnets woven or weirs mended.
His water and his desires
flow, swell and cure —
his *guineo*, grain and meat.
Suppose everything he lived by
were no farther away than the lower
rapids, between his village
and the nieces — a tumble
unspooling oxygen to a flock of pan fish
quick-silvering below dawn's tilt.
Suppose all sanity resided
as near as the screech of the unseen
macaw returning upriver.

EMANATE

Wet stone, the mineral smell
after a thunderstorm suspends

a bridge

across memory—not
the worn girders and trusses.

Sun spills, squadrons of steam
file skyward into blue fresh

as any mountain river.

But this silt—the fields
wrung of their fine-pressed clays,

lowland streams
saturated with a million

deciduous deaths—

this is *not* azure.
There is something carnal

being conveyed past the span,
a song or the fretting

of a lost boy,

the stringer of catfish tapping
his shoulder like a prism.

THE CAMPANILE

In the street three beggars switch their straw brooms
to the off hand,
pausing below a hibiscus hedge
to mop their brows.
Heat foils the town square.

The kid has grown too tough
to earn new tricks, or get his little dog to vault.
His dog would rather somersault in the wake of flies,
the ones with green wings
and marvelous crunch.

A poorer boy might
pedal his *Helados* cart up the cobbles
from the esplanade,
sell icy treats to the afternooners like votives to the sad.
No time to keep a little dog.

If the kid hopes to win trust
he will have to learn to throw his disappointment
in great whirling arcs.
The kid kneels beside his dog,
a pooch with terrier ears.

He holds a stick thinner than his wrist
ahead of the smooth muzzle —
a hurdle.
In broad daylight flies report
allegiance, idolatry across the sacristy of their eyes.

WISH MEAL

Dawned on her she was no girl.

Sour mash wove palpable in the morning air,
corn-fed hogs nuzzled leaves of the red oak.

Sun emerged
from a mackerel slit along the east hills.
She was a girl's glimmer.

To be unwed
in the mesh of duty and delectation required
a soul like a blacksmith, the anvil of insouciance
hardened by pounding fun.

She spread abundance
over the rumpled county like a comforter.

What else
to settle the draws and hollows,
the holding grounds of steeple, the relic
piers and wing walls teasing shadowy current?

She was no longer a girl, but she glimmered,
the kernel
seasoned, milled, sweetened by task.

CORRUGATED LONGING

I'm looking for a drawer
that holds lost socks, spoons
that went missing from
the old fire station.
I'm looking, standing
pigeon-toed, as if I
were still eleven
and needed to resist
this urge to
sidetrack. I'm looking
for you, crisp voice
of September crooning
a worn Stevie Wonder.
I'm holding this found sock
signaling a truce.
I'm looking for a bake sale
dish to cradle
surprise. Maybe
you've eyed me ranging —
know my haunted
stare.
The fluster of
corrective shoes.
I'm twirling a marred
silver ladle.
Hesitance —
I'm not much to recognize.
A gritty toy truck
with one bare axle.

FOR A SPELL

Point to Hood Canal as narrow and deep
as a trench clawed by glaciers
where spot prawns sweeten by the score
and silver salmon
eddy in cold-water ballrooms.
Show me a tendril estuary
sheltered below Mount Constance through diasporas
of winter tides, deluge and fog
where in late summer
bull orcas breach and crash
an alpenglow mirror and oyster larvae,
like 10,000 angels to a pin, enlarge themselves
in spangled drift.
Dabob, Quilcene,
Olympic lovers—all.
If August heat has pulsed faithful
late into afternoons.
If winds
don't chop the sequestered climes,
Pacific oyster larvae age
to spat these best last weeks of summer,
thriving on crab spawn, diatoms, kelp rinse.
Soon the oyster latches
onto a barnacled plank, old cleat, or shard
of vacant shell,
builds marble, flesh and *yes*—
salty autumn juice.
Grit and gush.
Out deep, the lingcod prowl their leopard lairs.
Leagues of salmon turn fervid noses home.

BREAKAGE

She broke heels at the county
hootenanny, he broke ankles
in a barnburner blaze, they broke

records on the frozen lawn, they
broke across state lines gunning
her flamingo dollhouse coupe.

Valentine's Day chill broke
water mains in the community center
where they nibbled and danced.

Teeth on his harrow were broken
from the steel crossbar under grasp
of a buried ancient stone.

The guy who promised disability
checks, by April, for her broken
millwright rode a stallion of fog

into a culvert down near Bakeoven.
The pulpit broke with tradition
to sail along the smudged tree line.

Her waters broke one night out
in Tygh Valley, while apples sweetened
in their queues, he broke his back

stoking confidence in mirrors.
Her mother called the vet nearby
to break a vow, to press the scalpel,

tug and knot his suture, dress the tear.

PUPIL

Slush tightens, the afternoon
gathers darkness like an Amish mother
spooling her skirt.
More snow expected.
No school tomorrow, money free
for the shoveling. Torsos of beech, small ash-colored tracks
dimple the expansive down.
Cows huddle, snort inside a broad barn
where sons and a nephew
scoop grain steaming from bins.
A sleet begins ticking against the husk of hardened
snow and from behind
the white two-story, smaller kids exit
powdery burrows like black larvae.
A man curries and brushes his Belgians.
All this luster empties
with the night, dilates, a pupil in some skull
of mercy.

YEARNING

Say the toolbox chose to be a wheeled
duffel, which stone alley would get traveled—
might these vise-grips catch moonlight, hold it
hostage to a travertine portico?
Could a bronze switch plate stargaze
ravenous from Table Mountain, propped
against the shoulder of an AWOL screwdriver?
Might this splayed wire brush incite shoeshine boys
slouching in San Cristóbal? Will the ratchet
suddenly turn to drive off a gypsy
palm-reading on a bench in Concepción?
Would these brushed-nickel faucets
embolden a Bengali ingénue to shed her sunlit
muslin blouse? In Prague, the dinged
crescent wrench opens his jaws like the arms
of a new lover. Quick, light is shifting.

THE WAY OF THE CROSS LEADS HOME

~ Traditional Protestant hymn by Jessie B. Pounds, 1906

The way is dusty uphill.
The way leads away from town.
The way interrupts your sacred week.
The way steals in on hours of sleep.
The way involves lying to barmaids.
The way messes with fishing and fighting.
The way fucks with political deals.
The way ravages your mama's heart.
The way scatters friends.
The way defies sedatives.
The way shoos off braggarts.
The way sets you on a bare shore.

DIVINE

We search for god
through inner thighs
and open space.

We feel for pulse
and portal
in faces long deceased.

We hear the snap
of expiration
as we climb the stairs.

We mull the wine
of absence
in an urn of piney air.

RECEDE

for George Hitchcock (1914–2010)

Skaters threw down rascally outside
a universe of rising floods.
Nollie, kickflip, grab
where
Royal Empress trees had lifted slabs
of sidewalk into bookends.
Drifting pigs retaliated against
a swoon of children crowding the sizzle
from the falafel vendor
but
a lone bicycle threaded a storyline
to rescue the sculptor pulling
lilies from her neck.
A beagle's prayers went unheard
under the madrigal of katydids.
Backside boardslide.
On the opposite bench
a snowy-haired gentleman
hatched robberies from his orange beret
snookering
fat men who steered briefs along display windows.

Hostesses
matriculated
through slatted doorways.
Skinheads reprised Valhalla tattoos.
Litter encouraged a meander
of swine below
the weediest stoops.
Fakie, heelflip.
A bus stop nurse arranged her
kerchief in weird blintzes.
The congregated shoes scuffed,
belched, wishing the ho-hum would return.
A land oozing blood
money.
Murk.
The town swirled its marmalade
of loss and luggage under
a biscuit lumpy sky.
The painter
kept inking
a riptide of ciphers.

DEAR GOD

I have learned, watching children doze,
to make fierce with the shadow of death.
My thoughts turn to you every spring
when flowers come too fast to really appreciate.
Also at Christmas when you bully your way
past playground guards to brighten
nights of rain.
I didn't get the part about you going to prepare
a place for us; why can't you finish
what you started?
I'm wondering if there's
an extended warranty for that survival kit
you sent me years ago. It sat
on the closet floor
so long the instructions must
have gotten wet 'cause the words run together.
Is there any burden in taking up
a small gold cross?
I have never forgotten the cigarettes
we smoked together riding our bikes
down the streets of Avalon
where they were building new houses.
How old were we? Ten, eleven?
There are afternoons
you haunt me when the fly-fishing sucks.
Neither of us has done well keeping promises.

DOCENA

We need eggs.
But it is Friday before Easter.
Not much luck lately with the farmer up the valley.
I load my nested cartons from months ago.
Don't have a lot of faith.
The yards I drive by *cluck-buk-buiïïk*
rowdy with bloom,
islands of stamens and pistils mobbed by bees.

A dozen! And another three I leave in the fridge.
Docena. I like that sound.
Docena, a cross-legged girl tossing gravel.
Reminds me of the Spanish word
for supper, *la cena*, not The Last — not stintingly passed
over for an angel's sake — but ordinary zestful, mightily
gratifying dinner.
These rose gold egg yolks broken for you.

PSALM RIVER

River looks for her name
in weak moonlight and strong, in the fabric
of a lost tennis shoe.
Say that I am
"Maumee, Au Sable, and Icicle Creek."
River has received eons of languorous snowflakes,
her slicks know the scrimshaw
of autumn storm.
Clam thieves, leaving her banks in a night fog,
whisper Little Skookum, Lilliwaup, Duckabush.
River funnels cloudbursts, rises
new to spring fever.
Her currents marry mutterings of August wind
with the sashays of cliff swallows at dusk.
River signs timber sales, bares clues to rail yard assaults,
buffets afternoon lovers.
River asks, "Who will I be
when all my names are stacked like a box
of old Christmas cards?"
Kayaks rodeo
the Upper McKenzie River's jade.
She sounds for a heading over basalt ledges,
sallied for decades
beside corpse-swollen side channels.
River steeps the bones of the ancestors.
Gathers from Santiam fallows
and Bi-Mart parking lots.
She rinses a corner of roof
collapsed in the shadow of a Touchet apple tree.
River waters edgy herds of Nestucca elk.
Steelhead stack like needles at the mouth
of River, inking her names.
River glosses the creak
of a half-drowned bicycle freckled by rust.
River knows the taste
for home, the final surge into salt.

II

ON THE BANKS OF THE WABASH

ALMA MATER

Wearing daisies on a red gingham
field a woman sorts late July
blueberries from a dull aluminum colander
and wonders how to tell her
eldest daughter Marian there will be
no more summers at the Finger
Lakes. No cheek-kissing mists
dancing off the waterfalls at Watkins Glen. Mac was
leaving General Electric
for the smokestacks of Indiana Steel.
No more perfect sunsets over Seneca Lake.
He's the provider, they follow.
"You're twelve, honey, changing schools anyway."
But who went to northwest Indiana?
Piles of iron ore, the belch of blast furnaces
for her piney, clear creek Adirondacks.
"You'll need a stiff upper lip to be an
example to your three younger sisters."
Marian from upstate New York would
learn to say Hoosier and Gary, Indiana
in a flattened cornfield voice,
would chirp "Valpo" for the high school
she'd never curtsy to or embrace, happier
being a bookish Yank while the dusky
fattened blue orbs were
separated from the mummy berries
at the edge of all she knew.

NAGOYA, APRIL 1947

from a photograph of my father

You resist tears
as cherry blossoms carpet stone
walkways with loss
the hues of *akebono, shirofugen,*
kwanzan trees. You imagine pale kimonos
incandescing in cedar wardrobes.

Six thousand tons of incendiary
bombs crushed aircraft factories, docks—
ignited homes.
You observe gaunt widows relieved,
overcome in surrender.
You have seen so many bodies.

I see your farm boy hands cupped
as starving arborists
salvage form from these living remnants
of imperial splendor. I do not see you
holding fertile flowers but
these ravaged silks of spring.

Your hands listen as if they might hear.

DIAPHANOUS

When she is a young wife
she hovers
as my father wields saws, hatchets and knives
in Doud's orchard.

Two years, he works this
promissory of apples and pears—a genius
to rows of cinder jigsaw pieces
through freezing drizzle or leafless Indiana light.
Jonathan, Grimes Golden, Northern Spy,
Seckel, Comice.

Fresh snow is rutted
to a plain two-story farmhouse by their old Dodge.
At the tall window this scant
dark-haired woman waits with an oval yearning.
White clapboard, white car, drifts of dazzling
frozen white.

Doud knows he is lucky to get a university
man with the grit of war
filing his temper to a keen edge.
My father knows Pacific tumult, distance
and a year of Russian.

But Mother is lost
against a coverlet of snow.
Marriage pulls, strains, jagged
as a Copeland hoedown.

She will massage her right eyelid
behind round tortoise-shell glasses, knowing more
in that instant
than my father can carry
perfecting his tools amid others' trees.

How numerous the hidden bumblebees
and stacked white hives
primed for pollinating her panic.
Mother will stand at the window
clutching her sides in a drab wool
blanket.

She sees everything
those two men on the tractored scaffold
size up and cut away, leaving
the better branches
of freeze-toughened buds.

Come spring she will erupt in flowers.

COME MONDAY

What made us think our fort
in the woods should be underground,
a double-wide grave,
the humus piled back over the studs
and plywood sheet?

How long could we have stayed buried
cradling our drippy canteens,
inhaling Milky Ways, jawing bubble gum,
a single, torso-wide opening
our exit and entrance?

The flashlights we borrowed
from the garage went dim in a week of visits;
failed to display
our smudged forearms, chins
or knees.

We deserted for church
and evening youth. Without bucket brigade water
our underbrush camouflage wilted.
Early Monday morning
coming to the gravesite we froze, glum.

Someone went and levered the top—

splintered the whole ceiling before
we could give
our dim heaven a name.

STATE ROAD 9 AND FINLY

Nobody glad-handed candy
at grandpa's highway grocery.
Someone wheeled away
from the Marathon pumps
without paying, once.
One week each summer
boys ages six, nine, twelve learned
to lust for fried chicken
and giblet gravy, imbibed
Three Stooges' *nyuck, nyuck,*
nyuuccccck cackles and Barney
Fife's blazing consternation.
There were flies to swat
on the screened door that
didn't quite close, eggs to candle
in the cramped stock room,
wooden coke boxes
they loaded with empties.
At five-thirty in the glossy
dawn, a bread man stole
the boys' rusty smelling sleep.
It was total grand theft.

ANOTHER

Our mother bends
over the commode, us boys part of her huddle.
The basin like a bowl of borscht.
Her shell-pink terrycloth
bathrobe is tight.
She spies the coin purse
balloon, whoever might have been
a little sister or brother,
and fishing it up with her fingers
nests it on the clean upturned lid
from a jar of mayonnaise.
She shows us a straight mouth and tiny hands.
This is what would be called
an object lesson, the veined gray placenta
with its beige passenger
gone rigid almost as quick as our young minds.

BLUE FERVOR

I.

A June night my parents
quit fuming over the dishes and
Indiana's immense humidity colonizes
screens of open bedroom windows as
dapper Frank Sinatra sings *My Way* and
The Summer Wind, "start spreadin' the news"
through the clink of our neighbors
playing horseshoes and flinging jibes
and flirts in the yard across the hedge.

My parents subside into nightclothes,
a housebound couple desperate on
our side of honeysuckle to make
a good account for Jesus' sake
and their always-empty pockets.

All the hurts,
jobs, tiffs, unpaid invoices—and reprobate
weaknesses—*are* massaged
nudged unguent, till ease overtakes

three boys too hot to sleep
anywhere but on sheet-softened air mattresses
on the cool, tiled, concrete floor.
The small fan purrs—side to side—like
a lookout on the prow of innocence.

II.

How shall the furtive be redeemed?

III.

Between our spring
choir and symphonic band come
winged chrome and fedoras. Come these suave
JFK acolytes, a Rat Pack.
I ogle as our high school jazz band files in.

Mom occupies
her land of *It Is Written*. Flustered.
To syncopate anything dank, more pendulous
than a big toe, borders on sin.

I roll, unroll the concert program,
loyal to my brother's balky
symphonic clarinet
but
I am thirteen, *spiced* —
will plow through hot dark dirt
to hear anything illicit, to hold haughty
April in one palm then the other.

IV.

Sheet music settles, the audience relaxes.

                              Mister Meyers tilts three rows of
rapt attention into his *1-2, un*to-3-4
                a swank guardian
                        coaxing protégés

                                        into radiance
            into Basie's *Corner Pocket,*

then *Lime House Blues,* always

his baton flicking
                        the black metal edge of the lead
                    alto's stand
initiating—   till he **he** *he* might cut, stamp
and sashay backwards into our
scarred
bleachers realm—while
            his furrowed young soloist ROLLICKS out of
                        the languor
Don't Get Around Much Anymore

                        and the horn sections
lean as if to lift butter from
cream—those creases
            in Mister Meyers' black tuxedo trousers
                        churning like blades, his starched

            white jacket damp, beginning to stick
                    the lumbar, his black bow tie stiff as bourbon,

            his left hand sparring, head jerking
to taunt time
                to a fervor.

CHAIN O' LAKES

A doll burned hairless
except for a cowlick
behind the right ear.
Skeleton
of the concessionaire's blackened wall tent.
Above char
the offending electric skillet
gleams like a guillotine.

Hisses of steam, restless
fire hoses.

The summer day loses color
behind a clump of locust trees,
and kids
who'd come to learn the crawl,
the backstroke or just to cool off
huddle, clutching sticky
ice cream wrappers.

Parents look to each other
through the sniping dark
wondering who will buy
scissors and dresses
and fresh Crayolas
for the concessionaire's kids;
who'll replace a banana seat bike
now this torpid week of August
has
burned into total loss?

Labor Day, September
sidling back to school.
How unctuous these weird
feet gathered
in flip flops.

BOYS DO THAT

She was kind in the one eye that worked.
Our hands were clumsy with cold.
It was sullen for late March.
Skinny tires rolling
the dimpled asphalt
had soaked us tailbone to nape.
"What on earth could bring you boys
here on such a foul afternoon?"
Brute effort unfolded our cramped limbs
to find her
just inside the diner door.
Her back was stooped,
Evelyn, Gladys, Maybelle?
There was scratch-made chicken 'n' dumpling soup
or beef with barley and several sorts
of fresh-baked pie.
There were age spots all across her hands.
One slice left no room to hesitate.
Pie, oh the pie I devoured
after guzzling chicken soup was
the *last* tart slice of green gooseberry
with sugar
like diamond dust.
Forty years from that diner
I linger on this catalog page devoted
to bare root gooseberry plants.
We were pedaling away from home.

TRYOUT

Happens
in the corner of a locker bay
before his damp-palmed
trudge up the bleachers
at the first Elmhurst High
Varsity Basketball game,
a freshman hoping to
show he's game. Hoping

now he'll man up
to sit beside or cozy below
those lightly freckled knees.
But his pre-game squishy
repositioning of moist lips
                    (one inept kiss)
well after the second week's
football locker-room
ribbing, smirks, when fresh
from a tiny parochial

school he learns guys
on his squad worry he's a queer
but in case he's not
they show him
                    how herky types
handle their mountain
of textbooks like a suitcase
that's lost its handle—
not like a favorite stuffed
animal he's gonna hold

to his heart.
Before he slides delirious
or grows cocky he hears
that jazzy, red-haired
ninth-grade cheerleader — she fears
                        well, he is *too* wild.
So she's breaking up.
Everyone knows how football
comes before basketball.

Brute formations
before
choreographic finesse.
And muscle memory.
Two revolutions left,
                one right —
there's a click, a susceptible
ease two-thirds of the way
to opening the lock.

INNOCENTS

Maybe this is limbo.
Name? —*no clue*, but I remember
a face, the swanky traipse and hoarse
giggle of a Roman Catholic girl
I liked, but mom insisted
would not love, because I was sixteen
she was fifteen, things
can swirl serious as heaven, hell—
in that swelter of
smiles. Early September,
ripe husks ripple, and hormones.
I could have protested,
witnessed to freer grace,
converting our rural chapel's shaded lawn
or a storage room pew
into desire's tensile rapture.
Most days
when I think of her
I'm wishing I'd simply witnessed more—
an olive inner elbow,
horsey freckled smirk, the narrowing
between her shoulder blades
as she reared to slug my arm.

GIANT TREE, WEST

If I follow the trunk of this matriarch
upward, will it lead to wisdom—tendrils
and grain devising strength from sky?

I stood under this ancient canopy
a decade ago with my father.
Mom's dementia a whisper between us.

We marveled at the luxury of rain, respite
from the saws and whistles catcalling
on slopes above my home, the sawing of age.

The apple doesn't fall far. Nobody spoke
of Indiana soy fields while hiking Oregon.
This sanctuary. Without marketable timber

or fruit. We stood on the narrow
Boy Scout bridge and sampled the flutter
of water passing below.

Bound away, I'm bound away,
far from the Continental Divide.
And now we span arms at this immense base.

What pursues me across the miles,
pith or sweetness? A bad apple.
Fifty years I've moved on his flat feet.

MAYDAY

She hears the rain tattering
in the magnolia
and wonders what her husband
will do with this harvest of wet.
Let bygones return
and build a new roof
over the breeze, let them excavate
footings against the gossip
of gooseberry and plum.
The hum of bees
busies toward dark as though
the humidity needed a flotilla of sighs.
She hears the moon
asking crickets
for the day's sales numbers
and the hospice nurse
flicks the tubing
to the morphine drip.

"THE SWAN'S METAL VOICE
RINGS LIKE A HARP"

~ Giovanni Pascoli

We come to a hospice room, convalesce
          to hear riffles of solace in the itinerant

harp where the hallway turns. Must
          our first tentative lick at the tangerine

lollipop lace itself in this corset of regret?
          Can't we just hum harmonies of swollen

spring afternoons, without quibbles, without
          Father Time filing his teeth, snootily,

between the saline bag and the sanitized
          curtain? We pause outside the elevator, look

to the player's fervent strum, uncertain
          whether our reconnaissance goes up

or down. The harpist builds a melody
          out of needles while we crowd the spent bed.

ON THE DAY YOU ARE DYING

for Marian Lucille Whitsel

On the day you are dying I check weather
reports, put a fresh tube in my bicycle tire. I close
the page on the stock market, play toss
and fetch with a black Lab for better than an hour.
All afternoon the sun licks the neighbor's
lawn as patiently as an old cat.
Sap in the cherry trees rises from a murmur
to a steady chug. Bumblebees waft to crocus

from Chinese witch hazel and flowering plum.
I rummage through an old poem, wash
a new pan; crush garlic, mince onion,
chop cilantro with an orange habanero—
mash the guacamole for supper.
On the day you work bravely at dying I cry
for the years of gardens my father raised.
I rub my often-sore elbow for all *your* pains.

You are getting in your gossamer slippers,
I am sobbing a little in the West.
I promise I'll write the IRS to explain, promise
to wash the car. I bow to daffodils for their
stabbing audacity in grim weeks of winter.
I remember your long bus ride
to watch me graduate. On the dying day, this day
I think about your cap and gown.

III

FERMENT

WESTBOUND

Behind a granite outcropping fringed with spruce
the train ran steadily out of sight.

Wrist for impossibly long days.
A bracelet of damaged beads, showcased in glare.

I knelt and laid my cheek against the track
while it hummed, praising the contoured fields

of sappy winter wheat,
those lilacs and mock orange the freight

buffeted yesterday.
I paused.

The linked saga scribbled tiny toward the far ridge.

I made my chest

a scrapbook for the stranded pickups and washing
machines, for the jacked convertibles

that sacrificed spinner wheels for Pampers, birthday parties
and heating oil. I yielded

to tarpapered back porches and the exposed
waferboard of unfinished rooms.

I pledged my afternoons to a drift
of perfume from centenary cottonwoods.

I trudged under a hymn of loose sky.
The horizon rallied gravestones under gauze.

WOOD FRIDAY

On my hands and knees I paint baseboard
to make nail holes disappear
as if this straight wood
could be fastened to rough plaster walls
without force or scar.
In a small corner of one bedroom I cannot see what I do,
head, shoulders and a marooned bookcase
block the only source of light.
I work by repetition and faith, praying
not to be revealed the fool
at this the hour of his gruesome demise
by morning's angle of illumination.

OREGON HORTICULTURE

Three previous days we'd seen highs
in the mid-nineties and it was only June.

The plant buyer said he'd spent hours hauling
hose over and across his parents' six acres

working to save the new trees and bushes
he'd planted this spring. He was glad

for Monday's low-slung clouds and cool air.
I wanted to ask if he was the good son —

the son who stayed behind, who resisted
the gleam of distant bays, the gravid tug

of new music and saucy-talking girls.
Or was he prodigal — but wised up soon

to a receding hairline, sniffing through the tang
of a windy landfill the sparse welcome

he might go back to if he picked his path
to the small town carefully, if he lifted

his gaze? "I'm the nearest one," he says.
"My older brother went to Canada in '69

and took citizenship. I have a sister
who sells life insurance in San Dimas.

My parents left the Bay Area a few years back.
Keeping perennials cultivates a little hope."

SITE READING

We see what we are when
we move what we have.

Pictures and knick-knacks wrapped
and shifted to a spare room;

trophies, a paddle and stuffed
animals banished

to the attic. Dressers we carry—
in an awkward

                  side sway—edging not to scrape

the doorjambs. A regretted stain, gashes
reappear as the rug gets rolled.

                  The sidelined mattress adjusts

hollows our idleness
excavated, fragrant

from the innards of every worry
and release.

The oils of our habits
printed around the missing switch plates,

now ghosts exposed
with some earlier color or grace.

SHOELACE LITTORAL

I.

Tomorrow the lancha will motor
this Hoosier boy across pewter flats,
around bends—downriver
to Limones.

A small shrimper will ferry him
to Esmeraldas, then an autobus
that tiptoes through ascending valleys
to a bleached mud square at Santo Domingo, crawling
ultimately past high gardens of the Quechua.

Two days jolting over a rumpled
equatorial quilt to cover the distance
a small plane could span
between a morning juice break and lunch.

II.

He will return, an older heart—

To admire silver expanses
of shrimp farms lining the coast,
a new asphalt road to Borbón.
The bruised efficiency of petroleum pipe.

Jungle sawdust still ferments
at this lip of the sea, brewing a rancid funk.
The noble guayacán overharvested, its yellow
blossoms regionally extinct, its grain tight as loss.

An orange tulipán towers high
over Estrecho Bering, the tiny sweets bodega—
a tide of litter laps the delta's streets.

He will save no souls.
Have no gospel—only trespass time.
He'll pray with every tongue he knows
to a briny-hipped goddess, intone his rumbling pecker.

III.

Whole tribes of chatter and outrage
have hatched, fledged, and flown
while these trees turn sunlight
into wood grain or a downpour into fruit.

See the raucous return
of red-lored parrots or cloud-towing
fleets of great green macaws flying—
dewy settling of dusk.

How will he carry this
in seventeen-year old hands? His heartbeat
shuffles a cloth-softened two-step
like the native cununo drum.

He wraps his recuerdos
for home, pads the woven *Cachi* baskets
with socks, corrals his still green
wooden drum in the corner.

Outside, homes
built of stilts, bamboo, and thatch.
Dueling marimbas punctuate oncoming night.
Pentatonic bambuco.

IV.

Are there quinines
to cure fevers of the outlandish heart?
What is the *Cachi* for indignant?
How far into his years can he carry a murdered sailor?

From the air all trees recede into tapestry.

Below the wing flaps,
this Río Cayapas molts to a platinum
shoelace, knotted high near the sunny
eyelet of a green gumboot of forest.

It dangles—unable to
be cinched or retied—a headwaters
loose and soiled for tanager, catfish, tapir, jaguar,
iguana. A vast common of solitary tasks.

MY INK IS BAD

Too jaded to weed my sweet corn,
shaken to mount the bike

I practice a phrase or seven
like a ventriloquist, the simper
of a beginning fly-fisher

casting loops back and forth
across smooth lawn.

Two fawns whose mom died in a clatter
of headlights, the riverside
reached but return stunted.

What sounds do these creatures
invent with her body bloating

on the shoulder of the road?
Is ink the bridge or this river
or the road that severs knowing?

MINIATURE

When we see best, looking with
our fingers and moist lines
of skin crisscrossing our palms,
we discover nostrils in the soft
bellies inside each elbow
and vestigial gills resonate
in the bones behind our ears.

We cannot be rushed, or bullied,
are always late but never tardy.

Our footfalls, running
to the dresser or trudging in
from the garage, become
minuets in dissipating heat,
fractal legends. The body
informed learns again this
desperate splendor of being
whole and wholly overwhelmed.

We make ourselves firsthand
a reminder: limpet, amulet, pinecone.

EMBELLISH

Stars, eagles and butterflies
we embroidered onto our bellbottoms and
muslin shoulders were too easily soiled,
then frayed. Some switched for pantsuits
or pinstripes as peaceniks were
ensnared to catch up, in ballet lessons
and IRAs. We conscripted deep in the belly.
We consulted ex-merchant marines and inmates
for signs. We swallowed our pensions like
sacerdotal lords. We bit down hard
on sticks or leather straps and learned
to bear the whir of needle, the principality
of ink. These blue garlands for his grandma
Dolores gracing his steps, this scripture of
Persian encasing your new guy's bicep, children's
names peeking from under the silk blouse,
the scald of a lion's mane inside her thigh.
Which totems mark the corridors of our blood,
what if the dream had not eaten us?

BRACING

I guzzle and guzzle the last
morning of bristling light this autumn —
again and again from my fatalist
stance behind the kitchen sink.
On the stereo Dexter Gordon tongues
grace notes to the head of *Cheese Cake*.
In the yard a season is shredding
notes, the sweetgum's spire
a cadenza of yellow to mulberry.
Woody stems stripped of basil
crisscross the cutting board. Seven jars
of tomatoes rumble from a canner bath.
The sink water is rosy with pulp.
Out beyond the gate clutches of goldfinches
filch, pester, free kernels from tawny stalks
of teasel; they'll fly the oil to the river.
The saxophone is an effervescing *brut*.
Sound ripples my hollow like
the grain in Oregon myrtle, this bowl
milled to mollify one vagrant heart
tipped over on home dirt.

FERMENT

On the darkest autumn morning I must
hope, pressing through an afternoon
of intermittence, come and go mist,
the occasional truck jake-braking, a dog wearing
his coat down to a sad meander.
Beyond my small river
cholera, hunger, polio
grab at children on both sides
of a faraway skirmish. Paralysis, pox
not peace. A lanyard of dust
two million faces long.
I should become their purse
of cool clean water, a shoulder bag of
fresh baguettes turning scripture and trespass
into the carbonic must it was meant to be.
Hire a road crew of apostrophes
so that anybody can have all they need
and some left over to ferment into new light.

WINTER FLIGHT

We could have been parting
a Red Sea, the Super Duty pickups idling
like behemoths, hazard lights
signaling breaths. The ridge above
a stole of Doug fir, bottomlands fringed in skeletal ash.

What smell
or snap eroded discipline, what fledged the breakaway?
Four cow elk and a young Bugle Boy
bull cross the road early tonight
to bed down

on new pasture, stitch our river. A sanctuary lit up
with accident and blown clouds.
They are not game, they are epiphany and pentecost.
The way home hums with distraught
headlights and soccer moms.

MUDFLAT ALLURE

Birds in the moist darkness.
A quintet of gulls sharks
for finger-length salt worms,
evening snacks as the tide
pulls away. Our lanterns
sizzle, flaring the abruption
of a blue heron making his
great-jointed ascent.

Working, at winter break.

Wool union suits scratch
young skin at the margins.
Our burlap bags will not freeze
while we kneel beside
dikes to rake for Manila clams.
In deeper water, light
gleams, a small tugboat nags
at the vast corduroy of a log boom.

Fog hangs in rivers of night air.

STELLAR

See all the pageant trees.
And stars.
Shouldn't angels
be accidents, beacons of desert light
twelve feet tall?

       A stranger
on the river trail offering pinochle tips
and sculptures
made of lichen and manzanita?

Nobles soar
two hundred feet in the wild.
Abies, from
abeo the rising one.

       Perturbing star.

The fright of a star chart tattooed
to the elderly
neighbor's abdomen
so she will know where to find
her soul in the next age.

MOLT

My father has no wine to spill;
he steps away from his table
to measure dusk's accumulation
of snow. Is this the down from
feathers, heaven ambivalent which
direction to tilt its wings, to gravity
or absence? He knows the uselessness
of letters and any worn tools.
The radio spools mayhem in Crimea,
destitute kids and distraught
grandmas in Aleppo. He has no
bread to cast. He wishes for a
sapling he could plant that would
grow limbs flexible enough for snow
and the depravities of angels.

GRAVEYARD NURSE'S RIME

Arm the shock paddles eleven
seismic apoplectic then serene hours.
      —glazed pupils, jumped
        like a dry battery.
Pinch, *jot*, flicking IV lines, *jot*
the Intensive Care—outside, icy drizzle.

Bums you met while waiting
for the bus stumbled on—eternal transfers.
Paunchy cauliflower faces
with no tribe but the curb, no totem
but a bronze Public Market pig.
Pike Place & Impossible.

Uphill an accordion bus disgorges
chill notes.
The graveyard shift of coffee
scuds your insides like a harsh tide.
You soothe the sow's statuesque flank—
gold in morning light.

Docents of the wee hours sleep
propped against the luggage
of dreams,
fresh bruises, hiccupped raw talk.
Consider these bright salmon
and fresh-cut flowers—craving.

You clutch ivory spider mums
for cover, drop coin into an upturned palm.
Gulls nip at wind wringing bluster
from Elliot Bay's blue salt-bones.
You can't go home again. You must.
All hearts rush away.

IV

FURROW & DRIFT

ADMISSION

An opossum comes
to rain-swollen kibble,
intent,
            feverish in the early dark.

Inside, the television
bickers,
            children are burrowing
into contours of story
and relief.

Dishes and residue of feast
wait on the counter.
Home work the young father
            refuses to learn —

his lady called in to doctor
heart disease
and noncompliant diabetes
            under a new moon
that has gotten to seem
so old.
            Armed with a straw broom
the father lunges
at the glass door.

            Opossum turns
and drags
a mangled hind leg back
across the patio into night.

STALLING

It takes years learning
to tighten the windpipe, south
of the larynx, on signal.
Son, this is what it takes to separate
warmth from what we eliminate,
a ritual withholding of air
then an opening twitch
below your tail.
Still you redden
rising up from the toilet seat,
the veins in your neck
engorged like sub-rosa tunnels,
rebelling against every labyrinthine
transport, our destiny, our discharge.

Upstairs the summons clerk will reach
inside her rotary barrel,
forming the jury with casual swipes,
names declaring themselves
distinct and as democratic as feces.
Necessary smirches on a panel of white.
I reach for my squares,
son, sending you
love at this pathetic moment,
knowing it can take a thousand nights
and dawning reprieves
learning when to squat—how and when
to hold your breath,
make your mark,
wipe beyond reasonable doubt.
Going, then going on.

CABIN FEVER

At Hood River, calls prevail between mendicant gulls
      echoing a lust

that guides our escape. Overhead the jet stream seeds
stratocumulus clouds.

      Rain-stricken bipeds we
shimmy along the escarpment. Gimme, gimme.

Skip the jewelry in ashram boutiques we'll sample wines.

These urges and Achilles tendons were conditioned
      certainly for some other brief. Shouldn't *we* retire

to a sunny town with Victorian porches, high ceilings

and waisted drapes? Above—the unsold condos.
      Below—gonzo cafes and outdoors sports specialties.

Everywhere anxious sailboards buffet the broad river's surf,
      tutti-frutti the wakes of grain barges.

A gull can yodel then coast above fields sown
      to red wheat, alfalfa. Or forage pits of plowed refuse.

But soil endures, our dark promise, our yoke.

Feudal—how we plot mercy or rebukes around a stone
      fence anchor.

Holiday garlands go up, rivals come down
along these glib, slant streets. A sunbird wheat farmer fires
      the heater in his motor coach

and a spreadsheet
      refugee coaxes vineyard cuttings in a blitz of light.

Salmon follow a furrow home
      below a phalanx of moaning penstocks.
Dams senesce with or without our river bluff vigils.

TIMBRE & LIFT

Years after she tired of hoisting
chains on the infant swing
higher than her captive
brother's screams, she preens
before a less precise mirror
to hoist the hem of her strapless

satin dress, the first strains
to a waltz a day-and-a-half away.
What glass or beau could echo
her true as the pupils of a child?
She does not know of the boy
with the halo of Cuban curls
whose belly is flat, and no longer

resembles the satin chamber
of a cello, though his voice as he
greets her from beside his reflex
camera and tripod has the tautness
of a bow raising tension like
a pert pair of dance heels.

AVIONICS

poem for a daughter

The morning sky is as blue as a Hopi bracelet —
September makes the vintage after summer goes.

I watched your sister back out to her life,
you a placeholder among college possessions.

Love is too musical, sporting, candid, immediate
between you and me to leave room for poems

which leads to thoughts about distance.
How you sang the alto beside me not a burr

on your voice until, listening, I *couldn't* sing
"Be Thou My Vision Oh Lord of My Heart"

my tongue trapped above the osprey's sticks
nested where an Adam's apple should float.

I heard how pretty you sing in the glisten
rimming the eyes of white-haired mavens,

who approved your song, your tanned allure.
A courtyard pine tree backed us, the weathered fence.

Buyers came last night for your sister's mare.
The mare nuzzled my sides for a missing carrot.

We spoke of anniversary picnics, mishaps, laughed.
I parted the dark mane, watched evening leach

light from the edges of long shadows
and understood how bird flights slim a treetop.

Who will stroke stories from our piano's keys?
Already I grieve your Martin saxophone,

September soccer, stutter-feints, elegant
midfield chips. The osprey roost is brittle, dense.

I tug at my bridle, a dull face going silver.
Sky is wide open, kid, and aching like an Irish hymn.

BIG SPOON

Stirring it up, or scraping it down,
I rarely leave the kitchen. I travel
acquainted with the clink of my kind but
remain unable to fit. I'll move sauces,
grains and stews —your broad *pinch hitter*
affecting barbecue rallies
in a lustrous October that cannot last.
Older implement anxiety.
I understand the grasp of spinster,
the two-mitted hug of a pig-tailed
scamp —but to *not abhor* this grim dolt
swinging me for a mallet?
Marred by work repeatedly,
still I'm ready to be lifted, delved,
to swoop over sputtering flavors.
I've grown accustomed to soaking
overnight beside strangers.
I know the cold grit of last night's
clams, the scald of each fresh start.

CREVICE

Indulgent spires of delphinium rise
above fern, salal and fast food wrappers.

You walk to the river, the water wicks
mixed skies and jauntiness from the university
on the opposite bank.

An Indian blanket trapped between rocks
torments the river
with reckless color.

You have seen these bathers.
Lost brothers building minarets of found rocks
on ledges in undisguised sun.

Students and pairs of staff pace the pedestrian bridge
in unmerited warmth, not ruby red,
but rosy
with desire to be appliances
in the vast passage of knowing.

There is no rudder to the blanket or the gravel bar.
You are more wrapper than fiddlehead.

RETURN POST FROM CANDIDE

No one bothers me daydreaming
between pole beans.

        A hundred yards away cars and trucks
        shudder past.

I pirouette my tongue around the name Guaranda, Ecuador

where an adopted mother,
school-mistress,
is dead—
three of her daughters flown
to North American lives.

        All have grown gray with itineraries.

Ladybugs busy the undersides of my potato leaves.

Doña Eloisa,

remember a foggy day you met a talking dog
while courting my elbow
on the cobbles we climbed
rocker-step
to the Guaranda open-air market?

        Santa Cherimoya, Santa Avena, Santa Naranjilla.

Co-op buses stenciled with roses,
skeletons, vírgenes, silhouettes of Che
caromed lustily
between rows of vendors and white stucco walls.

Festive horns
on poor tires.

           Those empanadas with cheese, highland
potatoes — ¡Que rica!

Graceful forward loops in your oldest daughter's script
resurrect infinite days,
           announcing death.

If you visit me this October in Oregon
           when leaves slough to valley soil,

I promise you a radiant slice of cinnamon apple pie
with melted cheddar
drooping over the edge.
           We'll ask the talking dog to sit by us
for a spell.

I sniff this huge Brandywine tomato.
Warm juice trickles from a crack
near the stem.

           You offer woven 18-karat chains —
famished for dollars.

Only the runt ears remain in these
spry rows of corn.

IRON SUMMER

The bath water
was bronze
as sun-tea
but little sisters frolicked
in it like
fresh snow, no wiser,
stronger
for the prick of
iron.
No
strain, no
moaning
for rust-stained blouses.
Well water summer
exact as a day
should end.
They
grappled
for wet toys,
invented
hilarity from the droop
or sudsing
of ridiculous hair.
Little blondes —
semi-
precious tiger-eye or
tourmaline
gaze.
It
was all we could do
to hear
choruses
and hope for
stacks of fresh towels.
Hope
such glee
gushed
from a new well.

THE STRAITS

for Kit Sibert

You wonder how to fill an empty cup
in a crowded loft.
There are no shoes to administer
your feet, no desert exile
or burning bush preparing to speak.
The painter's drips and skids mark no code
for the Buddha growing his cape
of moss. Your loss will not be clothed.
A cup full of shadows.
Weeks pass
like a pair of solitary picnic tables
placed end to end on yellowed grass.
It makes for easier mowing.
Makes the oceanside as hopeless as straw.

SUMMER OSSUARY

When greens weep chrome yellow,
I crane at the far ridges
hungry as a bull elk for frost, for the cadences of rain.
Squirrels hanker
to hoard half-ripe nuts in these tensile
sunbursts of autumn.
No scudding runs of fall chinook before storms.

I extol aluminum
July, lost radiant foil of summer.
Smooth tanned limbs, every dancing pendulum
of breast will be insulated soon in fleece.
Frugal glances
at lovers' elbows, backs and inner calves
harbor no late season flourish.

A chevron of sandhill cranes,
barely visible, calls a Sunday leaf-raker to prayer.
Across evening coyotes holler, yip, trill—gather
over a limp hare, and indulge.
My doubts jumar up gullies of hunter moonlight,
naked acrobats—
fence-to-limb-to-quicksilver cirrus from matted land.

I smell already the silty whorl of rain-clogged rivers.
December, January, fevers and worry.
I'm no trout to sleep for months
in icy current.
Certainly the sky is contagious.
Crab pots, ski slopes salvage only a little glee.
Vociferate.
How will I be fine?

TRANSIENTS

We are not here long
so we chain and hang and ring

these husks between pewter and gold.
We walk among ancient stones

and rivers costumed in turquoise and amethyst.
Our gaze is not long either.

So get busy with the grasp
of horror and glee, get while the incidents

of current and obstacle collide,
while the river foams for nostalgia

at the names she wore
in a cadence of April snow

or the ravishing forearms of June.
We are not here, we hover—

remnants. The conspiracy
of all that glimmers and disappears.

NOVEMBER ROAD

mutual forgiveness of vice
opens the gates of paradise
~William Blake

Shuffle through leaves as yellow as picnic plates
for one perfect Bigleaf while the black Labrador
heaves his tattered Frisbee. Again. Again!
Yellow foot lamps.
From summer gravel pressed into tar
by herculean machine, defiant
fungi sprout small strawberry domes. In drizzle.

Skeletons of butchered deer soften
beside the federal lane. Tagged, and hunted elsewhere.
You can collar, reef the snorting dog back.
Practice rounds, practice.
Rainbows of spent shotgun shells
and brass cartridges collage the road spur
above. Carry the antipathy away in a sky blue bag.

DIN, DINNER,

Here we are at the strewn table,
hungers sated, the napkins
rumpled or soiled like toddlers
after the first spring day.
Hemmed by pictures of laughing
or tyranny we've mitered and framed—
our escapes or executions
of ordinary land, lawns, blossom,
the unusually gnarled limb,
a bemused cheek. The check
waits facedown,
not for the waiter to return,
we're home after all and costs
are exorbitant, far far beyond
what any visited salon should bear.
Din, Dinner, Dinnest?
Somewhere lanais exist
designed to display domestic triumph.
Come back. What would it mean
to *de-nest*? The superlative case,
a ticket in hand
standing at the dock in the rain.
Birds fledging out of this orbit
of mussed song.

BOAT

For years I was your drift boat ferrying
one or all of you downstream to some
bend in the river, riding high through spring
runoff, shearing scarves of autumn fog.
I set your picnics on the water, posting
sun as bold and staunch as an onion.

Nobody recalls the boatwright's rasp
on my gunnels, C-clamps across my scarf,
the stink of yellow cedar. Did the torque
at first required to align my ribs decline
any gliding past that wild rope swing?
Even with this skid-shoe, my hull registers

knuckles of boulder, basalts growing moss.
You plotted my course between heron
squawk and belted kingfisher arabesques.
Rammed my bow into gravel and glister.
We've hauled away from root wads, shimmied
between shallow bars into favorite pools.

I stall above the moving claps of bug-manic trout.
I have faltered, I admit, against my anchor
certain nights in worship of stars.
We have not spared ourselves thunderclap
or icy dawns. You disembark one by one, move
along other rivers. I waver lighter with loss.

NOTES TO THE POEMS

Reside *Guineo* is the term preferred in coastal Ecuador for the type of bananas humans eat. Its association begins in West Guinea, Africa, includes the currency guineas and extends to the naming of Papua New Guinea. In the Philippines, the Tagalog word for banana is *saging*, which means from Guinea.

Wish Meal *Wing walls* are parts of structural bridge support, in this case a defunct bridge in which these pieces remain as relics.

Nagoya, April 1947 Nagoya was the fourth largest city in Japan during WWII and a center of aircraft manufacturing targeted in American bombing raids.

Bracing *Cheese Cake* is the title of a well-known jazz tune by the late saxophonist Dexter Gordon. He appeared in the 1986 film *Round Midnight*.

Shoelace Littoral *Cachi* is the name of the indigenous people living in the watershed of the Rio Cayapas in northwest Ecuador.

Return Post from Candide *Candide* is a nineteenth-century novel by Voltaire in which the protagonist Candide searched in South America for the fabled "lost city of gold." Unsuccessful, Candide returns to France where he works in his garden. *Cherimoya, Avena,* and *Naranjilla* are typical Ecuadorian fruit drinks.

Boat *Scarf/scarfing* is a structurally sound method of joining two beveled pieces of marine plywood in order to make a boat's hull longer in length than the typical 4' x 8' sheet of plywood.

ACKNOWLEDGMENTS

"Mudflat Allure" won first prize at the 2013 Northwest Poets' Concord and appears in *Concord, vol. 5*.

"On the Day You Are Dying" appeared in *Construction*, June 2013 (a New York online magazine).

"Bracing" appeared in *Cascadia Review,* May 2014.

"Site Reading" appeared in *Elohi Gadugi,* "Windows & Doors," Winter 2015.

Recordings of "Stellar," "Corrugated Longing" and "Nagoya, April 1947" are featured on the website www.thepoetryloft.net.

"Winter Flight," "Stellar" and "Transients" appeared in *Cascadia Review,* December 2015.

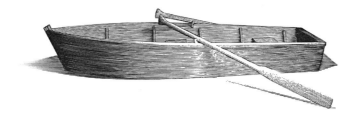

APPRECIATIONS

Thanks to Loren Wilkinson who noticed a spark, and to Erik Muller, John Witte and Mark Curry for substantive readings through the years, for listening and encouragement.

Thanks to PLAYA at Summer Lake for a three-week residency in the fall of 2014 during which some of these poems were reimagined.

Thanks to my Airlie editors for careful insights on the manuscript.

Thanks to book designer Beth C. Ford for giving these felt things visible beauty.

Thanks especially to the women of Poetry 1 Workshop who've welcomed me and my words into their lives and living rooms, for gently goading this guy to make sense.

Thanks to Sam Roxas-Chua for rekindling the obverse, for issuing it slant.

Thanks to Richard MacLean, Dick Barnhart, Mike Tripp and Dave Helfrich who've taken me to the river, and "let it wash me down."

Thanks to my family who endure and sustain me through my least artful antics.

ABOUT THE PUBLISHER

Airlie Press is run by writers. A nonprofit publishing collective, the press is dedicated to producing beautiful and compelling books of poetry. Its mission is to offer a shared-work publishing alternative for writers working in the Pacific Northwest. Airlie Press is supported by book sales and donations. All funds return to the press for the creation of new books of poetry.

COLOPHON

Titles are set in Arkhip, created by Igor Kuznetsov for Studio Design Klimov. Poems are set in Cochin, a serif Italian old-style typeface, designed in 1912 by Georges Peignot. Printed in Portland, Oregon on 30% post-consumer recycled paper.